Emotional Intelligence

Mastery Bible for Sales Success and Enhanced Relationships, Discover Why It Can Matter More Than IQ

including, but not limited to, — errors, omissions, or inaccuracies.

Table of Contents

Introduction

Have you ever looked at someone's life and wondered, "wow that person is very successful," or maybe you hang out with someone and you think to yourself, "this person has their life together." Have you ever wondered what it would be like for others to see you that way? Imagine people turning to you for advice, or you are the person that people envy. Maybe you dream to portray yourself in such a way that others can easily relate to. Perhaps you already have this ability, but don't you want to learn how to progress it? This book shows you how to obtain absolute success and portray yourself as an enviable character among others. It teaches you how to become a leader and progress your skills or learn new ones. This, my friend, is what it is like to have **Emotional Intelligence.**

Emotional intelligence is the pathway to a successful life, helping and enabling you to improve your skills, better your relationships, and learn how to behave in every aspect and situation that life throws at you. Maybe you have a short fuse and want to learn how to master calmness, or maybe you seem to mean or misunderstood, and you need some guidance to connect to others through self-regulation and self-awareness. Whatever your intent is in life, I can reassure you that, by reading this book, you will have your questions answered and you will not be disappointed. The objective of this book is to help you balance your life in ways you couldn't imagine, just by becoming more emotionally intelligent. Imagine that, just learning how to do one simple little thing, and your questions become answers, your life becomes balanced, and your goals become accomplished. Only one characteristic can shape your whole life. Continue reading to know exactly how to make this happen.

I have decided to write this book for readers just like you who have unanswered questions. I was once stuck in a world full of positive, friendly, and empowering people. My whole world consisted of, "if you do this then this will happen for you," or "if you learn that, then you can achieve this." I always felt like I could never measure up to the expectations of the ambitious environment and the people around me. As I studied mindfulness, I became less judgmental. Then I dabbled into what I thought I could become, and I never quite got success. Finally, I came across emotional intelligence. I was hooked. I learned new things about myself that I hadn't known before. As I put into practice all the things I'd read and studied involving emotional intelligence, or rather EQ emotional quotient, I realized people were starting to notice me. I became more goal oriented and confident. Everything that I wished would happen started to happen for me, and I was impressed beyond belief. My friends came to me and said I was different, but in a good way. My peers and even strangers seemed to be drawn to me. Although all this was happening so fast, I took what I learned and embraced it. I am no longer that scared innocent child I once was, but instead, I am confident and self-actualizing enough to make my dreams come true. I promise you that, by reading my book on emotional intelligence, you too will develop this power of awareness within yourself. Trust me, every bit of information is totally worth every second you spend diving in.

Emotional Intelligence; Mastery Bible for Sales Success and Enhanced Relationships, Discover Why It Can Matter More Than IQ addresses every concern you may have. It answers most, if not all, of your questions on why and how. This book is easy to read because I have written it in accordance to how someone like you can and will relate to it. I dove into the minds of the inexperienced and have provided you with the information needed to be an expert. You will learn the differences between your IQ and EQ and why EQ is more important. You will know how to tell if you have developed emotional intelligence and if someone you know has not. I have given you the fundamentals to succeed by knowing what to look for in an employer AND in an employee. This book was written for the minds of inexperienced beginners to reach their goals and also for experienced successful leaders. Whatever class you fit into, this book was written with your ideas in mind. As explained in this book, you will learn the very thing that makes up what emotional intelligence is and how to obtain and maintain it. Self-awareness and self-regulation are the two main components of emotional intelligence, and I am here to teach you exactly how to engage these aspects in your life.

If you still have questions and you are ready to have them answered, read no further than what's waiting for you - Chapter One! Chapter One will introduce you to the world of emotional intelligence and get you psyched to know more. If you are anything like I was, or like how I am now, then trust my instincts that I know exactly what your heart desires.

Chapter One: Introduction to Emotional Intelligence

Emotional intelligence (EI) is the ability to understand the way other people feel along with your own personal feelings. It is also used to consider other people's feelings before, during, and after making personal decisions. To have emotional intelligence, you need to develop three skills; emotional awareness for yourself and others, the ability to use emotions and apply them such as problem-solving, and the knowledge to manage emotions. To manage emotions means to regulate your feelings and being able to cheer up or calm someone else.

- Empathy is associated with EI because it relates to someone capable of connecting their personal feelings to other people. There are several models of EI. There is one mixed model that combines ability

EI and trait EI. Daniel Goleman, a science journalist, defines emotional intelligence as a variety of skills and characteristics that support leadership performance. The trait model involves behavioral temperaments and self-regarded abilities, which is measured through self-report. The ability model consists of a person's ability to break down emotional information and use it to explore the social environments. Research on EI state that individuals that have a high EI have healthier mental states, better job performances, and excellent leadership skills.

What Are Emotions?

Emotions are instinctive states of mind that respond to situations, moods, or relationships with other people. When someone's feelings run high, we either become a happy, blissful individual or we thrash around our house or room in an angry rage. In any case, our brains are wired naturally to override rational thought processes and favor emotional responses. Understanding your emotions is essential to your well-being for this reason.

Everything we see, hear, smell, taste, and touch are experienced emotionally before they reach our rational thinking. This is because all our senses pass through us in the form of electrical signals. Once the signals reach our brain, they go through a process of passing through our limbic systems before they ever reach our frontal lobes - the place where calm, rational thinking takes place.

Without emotions, the human race may not have evolved or made it this far on earth. We have five core emotions that make up how we think, what we do, and how we respond to circumstances around us. These six core emotions are fear, happiness, sadness, anger, surprise, and disgust. The problem most of us have is the inability to allow the emotional and rational parts of the brain to communicate in a balanced manner.

The Six Core Emotions

Paul Ekman, a contemporary psychologist who studies emotions, defines emotions as discrete, measurable, and physiologically distinct. Ekman did a variety of research techniques based on facial expressions and observed how people react to certain situations. Through his findings, he classified humans as having six core emotions including anger, disgust, happiness, sadness, fear, and surprise. Let's go through them now:

- **Anger** - An emotion that consists of the feeling of annoyance, displeasure, and hostility. Other names for anger include annoyance, irritation, resentment, etc.

- **Happiness** - The state of mind and feelings of contentment. Other names for happiness include contentment, joy, pleasure, cheer, enjoyment, etc.

- **Disgust** - The feeling of disapproval towards something, being offended by something unpleasant or unbearable. Other names for disgust include aversion, loathing, repugnance, revulsion, distaste, etc.

- **Sadness** - The state of mind in which someone feels low or upset. Other names for sadness include unhappiness, sorrow, regret, depression, misery, etc.

- **Fear** - An emotion that stems from a dangerous or unpredictable situation. When someone feels threatened, they will experience fear. Other names for fear include horror, alarm, anxiety, panic, dread, distress, etc.

- **Surprise** - A unexpected event, fact or thing. Other names include shock, revelation, startle, dumbfound, astound, amaze, etc.

Whether felt individually or as a mixed emotion, these core emotions make up the many feelings someone can experience. Emotional intelligence can also be referred to as EQ.

You can break up EI or EQ, rather, into two categories then two more sub-categories.

- **Personal Competence** - Includes self-awareness and self-management

- **Social Competence** - Includes social awareness and relationship management.

Self-awareness is when you understand yourself and your emotions in such a manner that allows you to understand what makes you tick. It is the ability to clearly distinguish what you personally need for your mental well-being and stability in your personal life. Self-management is the ability to do something or not selfishly. It is the ability to distinguish what makes you content in your life and the decisions you take with you to go after what you want and need. These two traits combined are what makes up personal competence.

Social awareness is having empathy for other people and understanding what drives them to make their decisions. It is driven by your ability to listen and perceive what others are feeling and thinking, connecting to them even if you don't feel the same as they do. Relationship management is the ability to use your social awareness with self-awareness in order to explore the connections between you and another person successfully. This consists of clear communication and effective conflict management. These two traits combined are what makes up social competence.

Together, these two characteristics are the basis of EQ.

Chapter Two: Characteristics of Emotional Intelligence

As explained in the previous chapter, there are four components that make up emotional intelligence. Self-awareness, self-management, social awareness, and relationship management. Also, as explained in the previous chapter, Daniel Goleman, a journalist, published a book introducing the concept of emotional intelligence. In his book, he expresses that EI is the ability to empathize and organize emotions within ourselves and others. To have emotional intelligence dramatically increases the chances of becoming successful and living a fulfilled life.

So, how does emotional intelligence feel in everyday life? Let's explore this question in detail.

Signs Someone Has Emotional Intelligence

Aside from the four components above, more studies have shown that motivation and empathy are what make up emotional intelligence as well. Motivation means to be productive and driven towards ambitions and goals. Motivation is the actions you take to become more successful in your waking life. Empathy explains the feelings that you attach to other people - feeling what they feel and making personal choices surrounding how someone else feels. Compassion consists of being a good listener, non-judgmental, and selfless. To be empathetic is to put the needs of other people ahead of your own; this reason alone shows that an emotionally intelligent person is seen as loyal and compassionate.

So how do you know if the five components of emotional intelligence are developed within yourself or someone else? Let's take a look at the signs:

1. You think about feelings

Emotional intelligence is the ability to recognize emotions and feelings and their impacts on yourself and others. Beginning what self- and social awareness, awareness consists of questions as a self-reflection. So, ask yourself questions like:

- What are my mental strengths? What are my weaknesses?

- How do my moods affect my thoughts and decision-making?

- What is going on behind the scenes that influences what others do or say?

When you ask yourself these questions, you gain valuable insights that you can use to your advantage.

2. You pause

You are mindful if you take a moment to think before you speak or act. This is easier said than done. By doing this, you will save yourself from becoming overwhelmed or taking on commitments before you embarrass yourself.

Pausing will help you make decisions effectively before jumping to a commitment based on how you feel about something.

3. You strive to control your thoughts

By focusing on your thoughts, you gain more control of your actions based on the emotions you experience. By becoming determined to address your thoughts and control them, you resist becoming a slave to irrational feelings.

When you do this, you will experience how to live in harmony with your goals and values.

4. You benefit from constructive criticism

When you receive negative feedback, ask yourself - How can this make me better? When you do this, you are trying to understand how you can benefit from the criticism of others. Criticism is a chance to learn and grow, even if it is not delivered in the best way. Many people are lousy at giving positive criticism, and, while you may not be able to control what they think, you can control your interpretation behind the words they use.

5. You show authenticity

Authenticity means to show credibility - a sense of genuineness. It doesn't mean you need to share everything about yourself, but rather, say what you mean and stick to it. Also, mean what you say, and then stick to your values and morals above everything else.

The people who matter in your life will appreciate your thought-sharing and feelings.

6. You demonstrate empathy

Empathy is a sign of compassion, having or feeling sympathy for other people. Rather than judging or labeling someone, you work hard on trying to connect to them, seeing things through their eyes. Having empathy means to understand others and their opinions, putting them before yourself.

7. You praise others

You are always looking for the good in other people, and you fail to see their negative side and give them praise for doing or saying good things. When you satisfy the appreciation needs of others, you build trust and respect from them. When you praise people, you make it apparent precisely what it is that they are doing good and inspire them to be the best version of themselves.

8. You give helpful feedback

Just like criticism, you may find yourself giving negative feedback, but instead, give yourself and other people positive feedback. Rather than hurting someone, you are building their self-esteem by encouraging them to better themselves and their lives in a positive, influential way.

9. You apologize

Saying sorry is often times humiliating, and it takes courage and strength to come forth and apologize for what you have done wrong or what the other party thinks you have done wrong. Being apologetic shows character, and people will naturally be drawn to you. Emotional intelligence, in this way, means to be able to let go of your pride when you value a relationship or connection.

10.   You forgive and forget

When you hold on to hate and grudges, never able to forgive, you are not affecting the other person but mainly yourself. The offending party moves on with their lives, and you are stuck in the past because you are unable to forgive and forget; you are only crushing your own soul. By forgiving and forgetting, you allow yourself to move forward rather than letting others define you and how you feel about something.

11. You keep your commitments

By keeping your word about the things you have promised, whether they are big or small, you develop a reputation of being trustworthy and reliable. Due to people's busy schedules, it is often difficult to keep our commitments, but as long as we try to keep our promises, we are practicing emotional intelligence.

12.   You help others

When you help others, you give yourself and them a sense of pride and reassurance. It is an uplifting trait that will keep your emotional intelligence level at its highest. The best way to help others is by using your personal experience and knowledge to teach them and act accordingly to their needs. When you help someone, you help them because you want to, not because you expect anything in return.

13.   You protect yourself from emotional sabotage

Emotional intelligence, like almost everything else, also has a dark side. When you realize and understand this, you will continue to sharpen your EI to protect yourself when people act out. A dark side of emotional intelligence consists of manipulation tactics or selfish tendencies from the influences around you.

Characteristics of an Emotionally Intelligent Person

One of the many reasons someone is successful in their professional and personal lives is because they have high emotional intelligence. Someone who possesses high EI has certain qualities about them that they practice every day to keep themselves as successful as they are.

Here is a list of qualities to possess to keep a steady level of EI within themselves.

1. They are not perfectionists

Being a perfectionist can get in the way of being emotionally intelligent because perfectionists take too much time to look for answers that may not be there, thus resulting in procrastination and shortening their goals. People with EI acknowledge that perfection does not exist, and if another person makes a mistake, they don't dwell; they learn from it and move on.

2. They balance work and play

All work and little play leads to high-stress levels and health problems. People with EI know how to balance work and play so that they do not get overwhelmed with stressful tasks. For example, they will put aside time for themselves for "me time," knowing that this will help them be more efficient when it is time to work.

3. They adapt to change

Having EI means that you are not afraid of change and can adapt well to it. Emotionally intelligent people know that being fearful of change is an obstacle to success. When they go through change, they make sure they plan and prepare before jumping right in, thus leading to the adaptation if changing surroundings.

4. They aren't easily distracted

People who get distracted easily do not have a high emotional intelligence level. If you cannot focus on the task at hand without first turning off your phone or getting rid of distractions, then you may need to work on your emotional intelligence. People with EI can work or concentrate without getting distracted easily.

5. They know their strengths and weaknesses

People with EI know themselves and what they want. They strive to do what they are good at and work on what they aren't. They understand when something is out of their element and don't put as much focus into succeeding at it; they acknowledge that their weaknesses are a waste of time. For example, if you are great at knitting, but not so great at building, then you are not going to go out of your way to accomplish building techniques unless you have to.

6. They motivate themselves.

When someone is self-motivated, they will go after their ambitions no matter what stands in their way. They are ambitious and goal oriented whether it develops at a young age or later in life.

7. They let go of the past and don't dwell on it.

When someone is too busy, they don't have time to dwell on the past or hold grudges. They learn to let go of what they cannot control and choose to focus on what they can in the present and for their future. When you hold grudges or focus too much on the past, you are consumed by negativity, which causes high levels of stress. If you have emotional intelligence, you will find that you do not have to focus on the stressful ties in your life; always focus on the positive outcomes rather than what is weighing you down.

8. They set and keep boundaries.

Many people with EI tend to come off as

pushovers due to their respective attitudes and kind aura, but, in fact, they always set boundaries and are good at keeping them. When an emotionally intelligent person takes on too many commitments, they quickly learn how to take care of themselves by saying no to others, making sure they balance their work effectively. They know if they say yes to everything, their stress levels will increase and their burnouts will happen sooner and more often.

Chapter Three: Self-Awareness and Self-Regulation

When we learn how to understand and regulate our personal emotions, we can respond better to the people and the world around us. Figuring out what influences our moods - good or bad - is beneficial to seeking or avoiding situations in the future.

Two important components out of the five elements of emotional intelligence are self-awareness and self-regulation. If we don't have these, our emotions will become a disturbance. A toddler having a temper tantrum is a good example of someone not utilizing these two components. Toddlers have temper tantrums and have not developed the skills to understand why they are acting as they are. It is their way of letting you know they are hot, hungry, bored, and/or tired. When we are young, self-awareness skills start, and, over time they learn, making it easier to determine how our emotions and behaviors impact us and those around us. This is emotional intelligence.

Self-regulation, however, is not the same as self-awareness. Self-awareness is recognizing behavior and mood and labeling it for what it is. It doesn't mean to change anything or act upon your emotions, it simply means they notice the moods associated with your behaviors. The self-regulation component means to improve and reflect upon our actions; we adjust our attitude according to situations or other people's feelings.

Self-Awareness

Self-awareness is the ability to understand your full personality and what makes you who you are. This includes your strengths and weaknesses, thoughts, beliefs, motivations, values, morals, perceptions, and emotions. Also, it allows you to understand how other people perceive your attitudes and responses to them when conversing and connecting with them.

If we practice becoming more self-aware, we can learn to engage in heightened awareness states, and our thoughts, emotions, and conversations will become more interpretive. We are creating the opportunity to make changes in our behaviors and beliefs.

Self-awareness development

When you develop a heightened sense of self-awareness, you will find it is easier to master what you want and need to become successful in your life. Focusing on becoming more aware will allow you to take control of your emotions, demeanor, and personality, making it easier to decide what your direction is based on your decisions.

To fully develop self-awareness, you must take time to sit alone with your thoughts and understand what makes you think and act the way you do. You cannot learn from reading a book, but you can take the advice from what you have read. Developing awareness consists of focusing all your attention on your inner self and directing your thoughts externally, then paying attention to the why and how.

Self-awareness is to be mindful of yourself, your thoughts, and why your ideas turn into actions based on your beliefs about what drives you. Learning self-awareness is like learning to dance. Dancers need to be aware of their surroundings and the way their bodies moves.

They learn choreography and steps through their teachers and books, but a book and a teacher cannot actually teach a dancer how to dance. A dancer needs rhythm to influence the way they move to the music, what their partners are doing, how much floor space they have, and awareness of other dancers, keeping in mind their teachings. Self-awareness is the same, paying attention to our thoughts, emotions, and behaviors and combining them to act accordingly.

Self-Regulation

Self-regulation is control of yourself, by yourself. It is very similar to self-control, but it is different in the aspect that self-control consists of refraining from acting on impulse, whereas self-regulation is reducing the frequency of our impulses by managing stress. Someone that has good emotional self-regulation can resist temptations and impulses that could worsen a circumstance. They are dependent upon themselves when it comes to cheering up when feeling sad or keeping their composure when dealing with difficult situations.

Examples of someone that has self-regulation are:

- A cashier or salesperson who stays polite and genuine when their customer is degrading them about something that is out of their control.

- A child who refrains from throwing a fit if they have been told they cannot have something he or she wants.

- A couple who walks away to "cool off" during an argument rather than resulting in yelling and saying hurtful things to each other.

- A student who chooses to stay in and study rather than falling into the temptation of partying with their friends.

- A person who chooses to eat healthily when eating at a restaurant with their peers instead of ordering their favorite dish.

Self-regulation falls into two groups, according to psychologists, to gain a sense of control over their lives and their behaviors. Behavioral self-regulation and emotional self-regulation. Here are the definitions of these terms:

Behavioral self-regulation

This is the ability to act in your best interest, long-term, in agreement with your deepest values. It allows you to feel one way but act against it or with it. An example of this is getting up in the morning for work, even though you don't want to, because you have responsibilities like providing food, shelter, and a means of a promotion at work.

Emotional self-regulation

This is the ability to control or have control over your emotions. An example of this is effectively calming yourself when you have expressed anger.

Development of self-regulation

Learning how to self-regulate is a skill that is important for emotional maturity and social connections. Maturity mirrors the ability to face emotional, social, and cognitive challenges in the environment with persistence and consideration. Self-regulation is much like mindfulness. Mindfulness is the practice of knowing oneself by observing behavior while being non-judgmental and without labeling our thoughts or emotions in everyday life.

Self-regulation requires someone to pause between expressing emotion and acting on the feeling or mood at the moment. This person will take the time to think things through rationally, make a plan, and wait patiently, carefully observing the why, what, and how.

If someone has a hard time developing self-regulation it usually means that the inability to express self-regulation started in early childhood. A child who has been neglected does not feel safe and secure which results in the child's difficulty to self-soothe. Later in life, if this skill was not developed, a teenager may have a hard time managing their feelings and act impulsively on them. If self-regulation is not established, it could or may cause problems with mental health disorders and problems with substance abuse such as drinking, drugs, or smoking habits.

To develop good self-regulation techniques is to provide structure and routine when we are infants to children. Routines help children learn what to expect, which makes their lives easier to manage, learn, and grow. When we become adults, we can manage self-regulation by understanding that we are in control of ourselves, not others or the world around us. It is not the hand you have been dealt, but the way you react to it that is essential for good regulation. In every situation or aspect of our lives, we generally have three options; we can approach, avoid, and/or attack. With this in mind, understand that, even if something is out of your control, you always have a choice regarding how you will react to the circumstance. The next step is to become aware of your feelings. Ask yourself why you want to run or why you feel like you need to lash out in anger. Restore the balance by focusing on your inner values and paying little attention to your temporary feelings or emotions.

When you practice self-awareness and self-regulation, these traits will instinctively become a way of life for you, acting as second nature. They will improve your resilience and ability to face challenging scenarios in your life.

Chapter Four: How to Improve Your Emotional Intelligence

As we have learned, emotional intelligence means to be aware of your emotions and behaviors. It is to be empathetic of the people and the environment around you. When you develop the characteristics of someone with this ability, you can become very successful in almost everything you do. If you don't have emotional intelligence, the good news is you can learn. ~~Put forth into your future and your desires for the motivation to become emotionally intelligent towards success.~~ Develop emotional intelligence further to become successful in your passionate desires.

Emotional intelligence (EI) is also known as emotional quotient (EQ). People who possess this quality can take the characteristics, like self-awareness, self-regulation, empathy, motivation, and social skill and use it to guide their thinking and behavior. This is, in short, what EI is; a high EQ increases your chances at successfully establishing your life goals.

So, the next question to ask ourselves is, how do I increase my emotional intelligence to become more successful? As explained in previous chapters, let's simplify it into four core skills needed to improve EI.

1. Identify your feelings and the feelings of others - empathy.

2. Use these feeling and emotions to guide your own reasoning behind your behaviors.

3. Understand why your moods change based on both your environment and events that unfold in your life.

4. Be open and honest with yourself about your emotions and make rational, logical decisions based on this.

Developing the Qualities of Emotional Intelligence

When you envy someone, another person has something you don't have but you want for yourself. When someone seems successful, the grass may not always be greener on their side. Part of being emotionally intelligent is realizing this and accepting that you are who you are. You are the only one in control of having what you have and getting what you need. So, let's take a look at how to develop and grow the qualities of someone who possesses emotional intelligence.

Adapt to and Embrace Change

People with EI or EQ understand that change is

a fundamental part of life. If you want to realize your full potential, you need to accept that change is constant. Don't run from it; be aware of it and embrace every possibility of change. When you do this, you will better understand how to stay capable of handling any situation.

Here are four steps to embracing change:

1. Write down your goals

~~Writing your goals down gives you reminders when you fall off track.~~ To keep progressing to complete your goals, is important to write them down so you don't forget. Keep these notes in a safe place that you will remember. These goals are essential to living the life you deserve. Remind yourself to strive towards these goals.

2. Choose things almost out of reach

Only you know your full potential. So, when you strive to fulfill a goal, challenge yourself to go slightly beyond it. When we are stuck doing what is within our reach, we never challenge ourselves to go further. If you do this, you will realize that you CAN handle more than you give yourself credit for. Once your goal is achieved, be mindful and reward this behavior.

3. Take big steps forward

Take steps beyond what is typical for you until they become habitual. Once your actions become a part of your everyday life, do them repeatedly until you reach a point in life where you want and imagined yourself to be. Don't let anything or anyone stand in the way of your goals.

4. Be stubborn and stay consistent.

By being consistent and staying stubborn towards your goal, you develop a trait within yourself that tells your brain that you can do anything. People that act with stubborn consistence usually succeed and make it to their destinations.

Be Self-Aware

When you are self-aware, you understand and realize exactly where you need to improve and what you have to learn. Your weaknesses don't hold you back; instead, let your mistakes and weaknesses build.

Here are five ways you can develop self-awareness:

1. Be quiet - Observant

When you take time to be still, in silence with yourself, you will truly be able to begin to know yourself and who you are. If being alone scares you, meditate and accept this of yourself. The only way fear can get to you is if you let it. Fear does not control you if you do not give it the power to take over. Acceptance is the best thing you can do to cure fear.

2. Understand that you are who you are, not who you want to be.

Some people know who they want to be but fail to notice that what they want may not be what they are destined to be. When you understand who you are, accept it. You can change, but change takes work and dedication. A self-aware person accepts themselves for who they are and deals with the present, making change where they can.

3. Find your strengths and weaknesses

Finding what you are good at can be the most complicated of things to accomplish. Discovering what your strengths and weaknesses are takes dedication and commitment, trial and error. The best gift you can give yourself is knowing when to quit.

4. Figure out your passions

Your passion is something you are natural at, and it is something at which you excel instinctively. To figure this out, you need to ask yourself—~~what am I so good at that others have a hard time doing?~~ what you are good at that other may not be so great at? What comes natural to you and only you? When you are obsessed with a specific niche or topic and when time doesn't seem to matter, this is your true passion.

5. Ask for feedback (positive and negative)

Look for criticism. Take what others say and think about it. Whether it is positive or negative, embrace that what others tell you is what they actually mean. This is where you can see how you are strong or weak. Often, we criticize ourselves too much, and the view from someone else can give us a different perspective.

Be Balanced

Work, school, family, friends, kids, responsibilities, and overwhelming tasks can be hard to balance in life. When someone has difficulties balancing all of this, they can become overly stressed and exhausted quickly. To be balanced is to be an excellent planner - a trait that an emotionally intelligent person acquires.

Here are three tips to create a healthy balanced life:

1. Rethink success

The world around us makes us believe that

success is difficult to obtain. You may read or hear that, in order to be successful, you need to have this or do that. If you want success, you have to know your passion or be emotionally intelligent. The truth about success is, no matter what you read, hear, or perceive about it and what it means, the only definition you should believe is your own. Ask yourself -What does success look like? Only then will you understand success and all the components needed to obtain it.

2. Identify your priorities

Once you find your definition of success, adjust your priorities or responsibilities to reflect your definition. Friends, family, and yourself are the most important people that will support you and your goals in your life. If you have pushed close relationships aside due to work, school, or materialistic things, it would be best to address this as soon as you can. Figure out what means most to you in your life right now, whether they are personal relationships or not. Once you figure this out, you can take action to make this your top priority.

3. Establish your legacy

It is never too late to start your journey, to create your story. It is not about the end goal, but the destination or path to get there. Some things to ask yourself are, what do you want to be known for? Who do you want standing with you in the end? What is going to be written in you eulogy? How do you want to be remembered? When you act on the answers to these questions, your legacy will be built.

Be curious

When you are curious, you will have numerous possibilities opened up to you. Curiosity means to dive into situations non-judgmentally and explore challenges head-on. It is to be spontaneous with a sense of wonder and control. Be open to new solutions and accept that you are here to learn.

Here are three techniques to help you embrace your inner curiosity:

1. Embrace the child-like mind

Have you ever noticed children like to touch, sniff, or taste almost everything they see? It's almost like they need to and if they don't, it bugs them. This is because they are curious. We all go through this stage, but, as we grow into adults, our curiosities are replaced with rigid and vigilant thinking. Try to put your mind back into the child-like curiosity state and ask yourself - How can I do something similarly productive?

2. Engage with a mentor or teacher

When you don't know about something and want to learn more, find yourself a trusted teacher or mentor to help guide you through the ropes. If you succeed in doing so, not only will you make a friend, but you will have made a valuable reference for your future projects.

3. Read, re-read, and read again.

Reading can give you lots of information. Don't just read, write notes and explore the endless stream of knowledge. Put yourself in the mind of a student and settle there. Once we accept that we are always out to seek advice and use what we know towards our goals, we can and will achieve them.

Now that we have gone over how to develop our skills in the characteristics of an emotionally intelligent person, we can strive to complete these steps every day. Use this information to be the best that you can be, and remember, never to stop learning.

Chapter Five: EQ vs. IQ

EQ, known as emotional quotient is the same as emotional intelligence - everything we have learned so far. It has the same definition as EI - the ability to understand your own and someone else's emotions. So what does IQ mean? IQ, meaning intelligence quotient, illustrates how high a person's intelligent level is. There are many tests provided by the internet or the universe letting you know what your IQ score is. So, as we know enough about EQ, let's explore what exactly intelligence quotient is.

What is Intelligence Quotient - IQ

An intelligence quotient is defined as a score calculated from a set of regulatory tests developed to measure one's intellectual abilities based on their age group. [1] In short, it is to estimate your mental age. The series of IQ tests you can find online are not professional, and while they may be fun, they are not classified as your official result. For this, a doctor would have to assess your IQ. The test, no matter where you take it, consists of tasks measuring intelligence involving short-term memory, analytical thinking, mathematical ability, and spatial recognition. Your results are not based on the amount of information you learn, but your capacity to take in information.

There is another test that is specifically designed for children that are called the performance intelligence quotient - PIQ test. This test consists of two main components: verbal and performance. The PIQ test determines where your child lies on the

---

[1] https://www.sciencedaily.com/terms/intelligence_quotient.htm

learning spectrum and is a good resource to determine the best education for your child's learning capabilities. There is a series of quizzes involving the PIQ, such as picture cards and puzzles. There are five different scales for evaluation including picture completion, picture arrangement, block design, digit symbol, and object assembly. It lasts for approximately an hour to an hour and a half and must be done by a psychologist or examiner in a school or clinical setting.

How to calculate your IQ

IQ scores are associated with factors such as morbidity and mortality, parental social status, and biological parental IQ. It is still debatable after almost a century of research that IQ is inheritable. IQ scores are used for educational purposes, a diagnosis of an intellectual disability, and job applicant evaluations.

If you have ever heard the term "they are beyond their years," this means that our chronological age does not match up with our mental age. The Stanford-Binet intelligence quotient test is proven reliable when detecting a mental age as opposed to chronological age. So how exactly does a psychologist or professional calculate this?

Step One:

The first step is to request to take an IQ test from a certified practitioner. An online test is for entertainment purposes only.

Step Two:

Write down the professional score in the following formula: IQ=MA/CA*100. MA refers to your mental age, and CA refers to your chronological age. Here is an example; If your CA is 10 and your IQ score is 120, the formula would read 120=MA/10*100.

Step Three:

Divide both sides of the equation by 100, which leaves you with 1.2=MA/10. The right side of the equation cancels out the multiplier of 100, and, dividing the left side of the equation, the result is 1.2.

Step Four:

Finally, multiply both sides of the equation by 10 to solve for what MA is.

What is More Important? EQ vs. IQ

First, let us recap - Intelligence quotient is a test provided to you by a professional measuring your intelligence level. Emotional intelligence is the awareness and control of one's inner emotions and ability to handle other's feelings empathetically alongside their own. There are major differences here. IQ is calculated based on your reasoning skills, memory, and visual and spatial processing. Emotional intelligence is not measured, but you can to identify, manage, and express emotions based on five components: self-awareness, self-regulation, motivation, empathy, and social skills.

IQ measures how high our intelligence levels are, which does not refer directly to our present intelligence. Even though someone may have a high IQ level, they are not able to succeed if they have no drive or motivation. However, EQ suggests that, in order to prevent misunderstandings, you need to be aware of the emotional feelings of others as well as yourself. If you want the best chances of success, then you will need all the support you can get. Without EQ, networking with people becomes very difficult, and you are only left with a high IQ.

In conclusion to this discussion, it is mostly found that EQ wins the race for importance in life. Although, it is good to combine the two together for a person to achieve their goals. EQ states a higher purpose because it is the ability to be aware of yourself and others before making decisions.

Reasons Why EQ is More Important than IQ

As we have learned much about emotional intelligence in this book, what it means, how to pursue, obtain, and develop it, what it looks like, etc. We can now look at the many reasons why it trumps IQ when it comes to becoming successful in life.

1. EQ has a higher impact on success rates

Your IQ score accounts for 20% of success rate in your life. Emotional and social intelligence, however, determine a much higher success rate when succeeding at achieving your life goals.

2. The ability to be patient

People who have the ability to pay for a short-term price today while waiting for a greater reward in their futures are proven to be more productive. ~~For example, someone that is starting a company or business, their goal may be to make a large profit, but for right now it is only to help people so their company can grow.~~ For example a startup company may have a long-term goal stating to make a lot of money, but their short-term goal is to be a non-profit organization to help people. To achieve this level of intelligence is the ability to put mindless entertainment aside for personal growth and development.

3. High EQ leads to healthier relationships

To live productively, we need to understand our feelings, the where, the why, and how to sufficiently express them. When we learn how to communicate our feelings in a supportive manner and understand the feelings of others, we can officially say we have healthy relationships.

4. Emotional health affects physical health

You cannot be emotionally healthy without being physically healthy and vice versa. For example, if we are overwhelmed by the many tasks and responsibilities we feel we have to address or must confront, we are filling our lives with stress; stress leads to a variety of physical health problems. We experience stress because we are uncomfortable with ourselves emotionally. Understanding the link to physical and emotional health will significantly impact our survival for achievement.

5. Low EQ has proven more criminal activity

It is scientifically proven that criminal activity is directly linked to the lack of emotional intelligence, as "criminals" tend to act purely on impulse. When a child is socially outcasted at a young age, they may direct their anger towards others and become bullies. Acting with fists rather than reason is their first instinct if they haven't developed emotional intelligence. These children grow up to have low attention spans, making it difficult to focus, which can lead to falling behind in classes and eventually failing grades. This result turns into a cycle of feeling unworthy and not good enough, and the person becomes more of an outcast than they initially were, which leads to making poor choices and sometimes criminal activity in adulthood.

So, as you see, emotional intelligence matters more than intelligence quotient, simply because having a high IQ does not mean you can manage essential life skills effectively. Emotional intelligence can help you build stronger relationships, be more productive at work and in your passionate career, and let you adequately handle life's challenges.

Chapter Six: EQ - The Root of Your Social World

Social World is a term applied to "universe of discussion." It involves cultural areas which are not physically bounded. Your social world shows how you can learn to understand yourself and your role in society. When you get to the root of your challenges based on your personality type, you will easily be able to overcome your problems and find happiness.

The social world is another name for sociology, so what is sociology? **Sociology**[2] is the study of human social relationships and institutions. Sociology has a broad spectrum ranging from crime to religious belief, from family to state, from race categories and social class to shared beliefs of a heritage background, and from

---

[2] https://sociology.unc.edu/undergraduate-program/sociology-major/what-is-sociology/

social stability to drastic change in societies. The study of sociology is to find the primary purpose of how human interaction and consciousness are shaped by the environment's cultural and social structures. Students and people that have studied sociology know how to think critically about human social life.

Emotional Intelligence and the Social World

The second part of EQ is the main focus around your social world - the ability to understand and empathetically relate and connect with the emotional states of others. Empathetic understanding has been a big part of many social projects. Sociologists - people that study the social habits of other people in the world around them - study emotions. They focus on emotional labor, and EI sits within their discipline. Emotions in the social world show

how useful someone can be in the workplace and in an organization's well-being.

By understanding and recognizing the social world around, you will be able to understand how to use emotional intelligence in things like leadership, performance bases in the workplace, and social media influences.

EQ in Leadership

Leadership abilities will help you perform better in school, the workplace, politics, volunteer organizations, and family and interpersonal relationships. When someone is a focused, dedicated leader, they are often very intellectual with their social and emotional skills. When you practice emotional and social intelligence, you will have an aura about you that seems trustworthy and comfortable. People will be able to relate to you, and, in achieving this closeness, will gain more prosperity in your life. In developing leadership abilities with team members in any aspect of life, you will learn to lift others up when something goes wrong, and celebrate with each other when things go right. Emotions are a big part of what develops these close relationships and help you achieve high, professional attitudes.

To be a leader means to lead. You need to embrace your confidence in yourself and direct or guide others to a "better" or more efficient way to deal with situations or projects. Leadership roles are designed to motivate and inspire, collaboratively focus, build trust, act with integrity, support, and to be understanding and empathetic. All leaders have a high EQ level, and this is what makes it easy for them to guide others, or naturally take the lead in the way of management.

EQ in Social Media Marketing

To become a social media marketer, you need one key ingredient to not feel as if you are struggling with getting the results you want - emotional intelligence. Studies show that 80% of marketers assume they know their target market, but, in reality, 63% of consumers say their brands do not understand them. An emotional quotient is an ingredient to why consumers feel differently than marketers in this aspect.

The first thing you need to do if you are a social media marketer is to listen to your target audience. Understand them on a deeper level. Figure out their habits, what they like, what they don't, what they can relate to and where they want your brand to go. When you know this information, you can develop and grow your company by accommodating to their needs. Part of having EQ is knowing that your brand and your business are not just about what you want; they are mainly about what your target audience expects and needs. You are behind the scenes while your audiences are the main performers.

92% of consumers want to be able to relate, so they know what they are getting into. If you are a beginner, your main focus is to connect to the social world around you. Do this by telling a story. When your consumers want to connect with you, their interest piques, but how do you get them to stay? Help them. That is the only answer: people like to be helped. Reach out to them through the connections you have made. When your customer has made complaints or concerns, address them immediately and effectively. You will have customers coming back once they feel they have been heard.

EQ in the Workplace

EQ is a hot topic in psychology and the world of business along with many other prospects in life. EQ defines how you use your emotional mind to make decisions, solve problems, and communicate with others. All these traits revolving around EQ are the most important traits needed to be an excellent employee or employer. Emotional quotient plays an important role in how employees interact with co-workers and manage stress and conflict as an overall performance level on the job.

Emotional intelligence is critical to your success because it isn't just for employees, but employers and leaders of huge companies as well. It teaches a leader how to cooperate and react accordingly with their teammates and with their customers. EQ teaches employees how to be respectable and co-habitat with other people around them, even when they don't get along or agree.

Based on this information, having emotional intelligence can lead to better business, better response tactics, gains in empathetic behavior, and can make the person proficient in the skill listen, reflect, and respond constructively.

Social Intelligence

Social intelligence is different than emotional intelligence because, as EI mainly focuses on yourself and the emotions of others, SI is developed by using EQ strategies. Social intelligence, for example, is something you develop over time when you have experiences with people and make mistakes or achievements in social settings. Some other terms to define SI are "street smarts," or "common sense."

There are five key elements of social intelligence. Let's address them now:

1. Conversational skills

When you find someone that knows how to "work a room," then you will most likely find out they have high social intelligence. When someone is socially intelligent, it is easy for them to hold conversations with a large group of people effectively.

2. Knowledgeable in social roles, rules, and scripts

SI people learn and know how to play distinct social roles. They will be perceived as socially sophisticated and wise, as they know how to "play the game" of social interaction. This consists of changing the way they talk and listen, depending on who they are conversing or interacting with.

3. Listening and interpreting skills

They are great listeners. Have you ever walked away from a conversation and felt good or had a different feeling from before you talked to them? This is because they took the time to listen and interpret what you had to say.

4. Understanding what makes someone upset

Social intelligence means not only to listen but to watch and be observant. People with social intelligence carefully analyze the way you move, talk, and perform and then address you accordingly. When they understand how someone behaves, they can fine-tune their attitudes and act upon what you are thinking and feeling.

5. Impression management skills

When someone wants to be exceptionally skilled in SI, they observe how they feel and are continuously watching the impressions they make on their peers. For example, someone who has high-impression management skills shows you what they want you to see to make certain impressions. This is the most complex element of SI.

The only real way you can develop social intelligence if you don't already have it is by experiencing social activity. Surround yourself by a therapist or motivational speaker, watch their behaviors, and then learn from them. You will make mistakes, but as you develop SI, you will find the world and society will slowly fall at your feet and be drawn to you.

Chapter Seven: Emotional Intelligence in Relationships

It is said that emotional and social intelligence can determine the success or failure rate of our personal relationships. The only example of when this does not happen is between parent and child connections; otherwise, it is very rare to find a relationship that shows no expectations of one side or the other. Similarly, the success rate of an intimate relationship can be impacted mainly by the compatibility of the two individuals' levels of emotional intelligence. EQ is equal to other characteristics, such as background and values, in determining if a relationship will be successful.

However, even if two individuals show that their EQ levels are similar, that doesn't mean they are compatible with each other. One partner may have a high level of communication and a low level of memory, whereas the other partner may have low levels of communication and strength in memory. In the total aspects of levels, the two may be incompatible even if their EQ scores show similarity.

Another aspect that may show two similar emotionally intelligent people may not be compatible is based on experiences. ~~If one person is charming and the other has had bad experiences with their past relationships because their ex was charming, it may not work out.~~ For example, if your potential partner is charming but your ex was also charming and it didn't work out between you and your ex, then you may second guess a charming behavior with anyone.

Why Emotional Intelligence in Relationships Matters

Aside from the ingredients of what makes a healthy relationship, like trust, honesty, and communication, emotional intelligence is what makes a healthy relationship also. Often, this ingredient is missed. Emotional intelligence matters in a relationship because it is the ability to understand your partner's feelings, and be able to reason with them in difficult times. Some people are natural empaths, and others need to learn this skill. Regardless of EI or EQ, it is beneficial for a couple's happiness and well-being to learn these skills.

Here are five reasons EI matters in a relationship:

1. Empathizing with each other

When you can successfully put your needs

aside for your partner and sympathize how they feel above your own emotions it is called empathy. When you are empathetic toward your partner, your relationship grows stronger, making your partnership almost unbreakable. When we are seen and understood, we create a bond with each other. ~~Having a partner that is in tune with us makes us feel as though we complement each other.~~ Having a partner that understands us on a deeper level is called being empathetic for each other's feelings. It is good to have a partnership that complements one another on a deeper level.

2. You can have a meaningful conversation without breaking into arguments

It is said that when someone is emotionally intelligent, they are able to take criticism (positive and negative feedback) and turn it into a learning experience. The reason this is an excellent trait to have during a relationship is that constructively expressing our feelings means we can say what needs to be said non-judgmentally, making for better communication. When our partner addresses their concerns with us in a healthy manner, this is an example of having a meaningful conversation without escalating effects.

3. Vulnerability comes naturally with each other

Weakness is one of the scariest things people face when it comes to connecting with someone. It is good to be vulnerable because it helps us connect on a deeper level with our spouse or partner. Being emotionally intelligent means that you know when and how to start being vulnerable. Once someone becomes susceptible, it can be difficult to continue being unguarded. This is why EI is an exceptional quality to have: "If a partner is able to identify a pattern in which they feel an emotion that makes them vulnerable and expresses that to you, they demonstrate emotional intelligence and a pulse on the relationship."[3]

4. Feelings can be directly expressed

When someone shows passive aggressiveness or gives the silent treatment, it shows signs that this person may not be emotionally intelligent. On the other hand, when someone can verbally express what they mean and show how they feel through their actions, it shows emotional intelligence. No one can read minds, so when you represent the way you feel and talk about solutions to your problems, your needs will and should be met. One of the biggest

---

[3] Christie Tcharkhoutian,

accomplishments for a relationship is to authentically share how you feel and be able to ask for what you need from your spouse or partner. Part of being emotionally intelligent in your relationship lets you be completely aware of these needs so you can fully express your feelings with your partner.

5. Apologies become more acceptable, making it easier to make-up quicker

Most people are full of pride, and so it can be difficult to say sorry. Being emotionally intelligent means that we can fully accept that when we are wrong, we will own up to our mistakes and apologize to the ones we love. If you cannot say sorry to your partner when you are wrong or have made a mistake, you show clear signs of not being emotionally intelligent, and resentment slowly builds up, leaving the relationship to fill with gradual poison. Someone who accepts their mistakes and owns up to them would rather make amends and be close rather than be right and risk pushing their intimate partner away.

In conclusion, having emotional intelligence in a relationship lets you be aware of your partner's needs and to help manage conflict in a healthy way. It allows you to understand each other, bringing you closer together on a deeper field. EI in a relationship enables you to decipher the difference between having a productive argument and having a fight that gradually brings you to end the relationship.

Fix Your Relationship Using Emotional Intelligence

If your relationship seems to be falling apart, it is most likely because the honeymoon stage has ended and things have gotten more serious. This is the stage where your differences come out, and you start to learn how you can make this relationship turn into a healthy, happy life-long commitment. Your emotional EQ plays an important role in determining whether your relationship will last. Just because you and your spouse don't see eye to eye all the time, or that you deal with your emotions differently, it doesn't mean you walk away. You need to spend time figuring out how to relate to each other.

We have discussed why having emotional intelligence in your relationship is crucial, but let's now figure out how you can work on and improve your EQ to make you both feel better about each other.

1. Don't disapprove of "ugly" feelings

When someone expresses jealousy, depression,

or anger in a relationship, it can be unhealthy and destroy a relationship rather than fix it. Everyone has a darker side to their personalities; whether they choose to act on their dark impulses or not is the concern. Being able to embrace your spouse's shadow-self - dark side - means to accept their faults as a whole and vice versa. Even though you may fight a lot, if you accept their darker side and negative traits, you set your relationship up for success. Acknowledge this early in the involvement, that the dark stuff is going to happen regardless, so, be positive about it and address it accordingly. Work together with your shadow selves.

2. Discuss the difficult stuff early

No one wants to address their difficult stories upon meeting or getting to know each other, but the fact is that there is never really a good time to talk about the challenging stuff. The sooner you get this out of the way, the more successful you, as a couple, will be. When your partner knows what triggers you, or what emotions you are bothered by, this sets boundaries and lets your partner know beforehand what to do and what not to do. Be careful not to address it aggressively as this may come off as you are controlling. Instead, think about addressing your concerns and setting your relationship for a long-term commitment. If you or your spouse cannot work together based on your boundaries, then why go for the "long haul" when it's probably best to stay friends?

3. Pay attention to your tone

The way you talk and how you pitch your tone is a strong communication tactic that, depending on the tone you use, will depend on the mood or direction your conversations will go. The way we talk to people indicates whether or not our relationships are to be successful or not. Having a high EQ has a lot to do with this, as part of its definition is to be self-aware of the way you portray your actions, emotions, and voice. An example of this is if you and your significant other are having a disagreement, and you feel disrespected in any way, or vice versa, having a frustrated, annoyed or negative tone in response will likely make the situation worse. Now, if you were to address their words, or feelings with a calm, attentive tone, without being a "pushover," the conflict will likely be solved faster.

4. Be pragmatic about what you expect

Whether you are starting out in a relationship or you are months or years into it, it is crucial to set expectations. When both parties know where each other stands, it sets the foundation for a healthy relationship. Careful, though, setting expectations too high can cause major conflict. Also, do not make your expectations unrealistic, and always address your expectations with your spouse so that there is no miscommunication. As you develop an understanding of each other and get to know each other more, this will come more naturally to both parties. People that have high EQ levels are more likely to have more patience and be able to move on without putting as much effort into making things work with the person they love. In the same sense, developing your EQ doesn't mean you are superior, but that you are willing to learn and grow together as a team.

5. Listen to understand: Hear what your partner is saying

This may sound repetitive, but it is crucial to enhance your relationship's EQ. It is one thing to listen and another thing to be heard and interpret what the other person is saying. When you listen, you can get distracted easily, and it can be harder for you to understand and connect with your partner. If you actually take the time to interpret what your spouse is saying to you without distractions, then you are taking the time to hear and process the conflict, making it easier to solve the problem. Having a high EQ together makes you be able to do this. Listen without judgment, and react without anger. When you fully listen, you are listening without thoughts of your own spiraling inside your head. You are not listening to respond but rather listening to be empathetic. Finally, resulting in working it out together in the end.

6. Don't run from arguments. Be okay with disagreements and differences

There is an amount of arguing, fighting, and disagreeing that can be healthy. When you fight or argue with your spouse, it shows that you care about yourself and the other person. If we didn't take the time to "duke it out," then we would show a lack of interest in the other person. Fighting can be healthy because it shows each other what is right, wrong, or triggering. Sometimes loving each other needs to be about being heard and wearing yourselves out to ignite the spark again. If you don't take the time to fight, your values and the problems you are experiencing can build and build, leading to one big explosion. Fighting can lessen these explosions and make you both come out understanding more from each other's point of views.

7. Know your strengths, work on your weaknesses

An excellent way to grow your relationship's EQ is to know your strengths and weaknesses as well as your partner's. What is important to know about each other is, who has a shorter fuse than the other? Who is more patient? Who vents rather than letting things go more? When you both understand how you react, you disclose vulnerability, which creates emotional intimacy.

Chapter Eight: Why Emotional Intelligence is Crucial for Success

Having a high IQ score, being able to decipher what it is in life you want, or being able to apply knowledge to your passions is not all that is required for a successful life. Emotional intelligence and everything we have learned so far explains that the way you carry yourself based on the way you think and feel is what it truly means to become an accomplished individual. Having a high emotional quotient enables you to be communicative in such a way that both parties of the conversation become fulfilled because it means to express yourself and them empathetically. So, if you are good at managing stress, resolving conflict, and thinking before you speak, then you know what it is like to be emotionally intelligent.

Low Emotional Intelligence

Before moving onto what makes an emotionally intelligent person successful, we may learn better if we understand the many ways that a person may not be emotionally intelligent. It is not necessarily a bad thing to not have emotional intelligence since this can be a learned skill, but it is good to know the signs so you can work on developing your emotional intelligence skills. If these signs sound like you, remember not to beat yourself up for what you don't have, but, remember, you can be successful if you put your full effort in your everyday life.

Here are signs you have low emotional intelligence:

1. You have a short fuse, getting into many arguments

Individuals with low EQ levels struggle to understand the way other people feel, and so they find themselves arguing a lot. These people will pick a fight with friends, family, co-workers, employers, and random strangers. They have a hard time accepting they are wrong, and so they only find their personal beliefs to be correct. This is because they lack interest in wanting to relate to others.

2. You cannot or have a hard time relating to other people

Alongside argumentative individuals, they are entirely oblivious to how others feel. They have a hard time knowing why their spouses or co-workers may be angry or irritated. Someone doesn't have to be irritated or annoyed with you for you to understand what they feel, but it's the fact that you feel no emotion or empathy towards the way someone else is feeling that defines your lack of emotional intelligence. People naturally have expectations of others to know how to tell the signs of when they are upset. If you have no tendency to understand how someone is feeling, you probably have a low EQ.

3. You think other people are overly sensitive

If you find yourself making "too soon" jokes over something that is inappropriate, like at a funeral or after a tragic event, and everyone around you becomes offended, this shows low EQ. Individuals with low EQ find others to be overly sensitive, rather than thinking they are being inappropriate. Since this type of individual has a hard time understanding the emotions of others, they tend to act this way, not thinking anything is wrong.

4. You are focused around the way you think rather than listening to other perspectives

If you have low EQ, you are unwilling to see the views of others because you feel as though you are always right. You don't take criticism lightly, and you feel threatened or offended when someone tries to prove you wrong. These people are typically negative and quite often critical of others' feelings.

5. You constantly blame others

When you don't understand your own feelings, then you may have a difficult time understanding how your actions may lead to the problems you created. Someone with low emotional intelligence blames others for their actions as a first instinct. If this sounds like you, you may find yourself making excuses like someone else made you do what you did, insisting you had no other choice. When you cannot take responsibility for your actions, you may feel bitter and victimized, as though everyone is out to get you.

6. You are unable to cope with emotionally-charged situations

Emotional situations are difficult to be around because you may not be emotionally censored to handle such circumstances. These individuals may walk away from emotionally-charged situations because they are not willing to deal with such conflicts. They may seem guarded and reserved as well.

7. You have emotional outbursts

People with low EQ have a hard time understanding their emotions and what sets them off, and this in result may have sudden emotional outbursts. If you notice yourself getting angry for no reason, have a strong urge to cry out of nowhere, or feel off or lonely, you are experiencing an emotional outburst.

8. You have a hard time keeping lasting friendships

The reason someone with low EQ may have a hard time obtaining and maintaining friendships is that they appear disagreeable and insensitive. When you can't relate to someone like this, you are not about to spend the time trying to keep a friend that has no empathy for the way you feel. They may seem disrespectful and selfish. Close relationships require give-and-take, sharing emotions, compassion, and emotional support. All of these aspects define someone with emotional intelligence.

Now that we have discussed what someone with low emotional intelligence looks like, we can move on to how a great deal of success revolves around EQ.

Why Emotionally Intelligent People Succeed

Studies show that there are three primary reasons that people and businesses fail: difficulty in handling change, inability to work with people or as a team, and poor interpersonal relations. Research has tested 515 business executives, and those that had a higher EQ showed that they were more successful than the executives that had lower EQ. Other studies from the "Carnegie Institute of Technology" show that 85% of financial success was due to skills in human engineering, personality, communication abilities, negotiation tactics, and leadership skills. Their results showed that only 15% was due to technical ability, which proves that a much higher percentage is related to emotional intelligence.

Most research revolving success around emotional intelligence has tested solely on executive leadership levels. The higher up the company, the more crucial EQ comes into play, as it dramatically impacts the level of success throughout the entire organization. An example of how this works is a study by McClelland in 1999, showing that supervisors in manufacturing that listened better lost-time accidents decreased by 50% and grievances went from fifteen to three per year. The plant itself surpassed productivity goals by $250,000.

This principle applies to all areas of life, at work and in relationships. People want to work with other people that are easy to get along with and who are easy to communicate with on an intellectual level. We want to be uplifted by leaders and work alongside people who can be constructive when resolving a conflict. The people who acquire these traits are successful because of their abilities to act appropriately in every aspect.

Hiring an Emotionally Intelligent Person

If you are an employer looking to hire someone that has the potential to make your business better or seems to have a good foundation of what they think is successful, then you definitely want to aim for someone that has emotional intelligence.

The first thing you should look for in an employee that has emotional intelligence is their self-awareness. These people will deal honesty within themselves and with you. They have a good understanding of their goals and can give a clear road map regarding how they are going to achieve them. They are confident and aware of their limitations, resulting in their abilities to not set themselves up to fail. To notice a self-aware person, listen to how they talk about themselves in a non-defensive manner. When questioning them, ask them to tell you about a time where they got carried away by their emotions and later regretted their actions. A self-aware person will be straightforward and honest. Someone who is not self-aware will avoid or stall and seem irritated by the question.

The second thing to look for when hiring an emotionally intelligent person is the ability to self-regulate emotions. When someone is good at self-regulating their feelings, they will act appropriately to situations rather than on their impulses. When someone acts on their impulses, they create havoc, disruptions, and lasting negative feelings to those around them. When interviewing, look for someone who takes little time to reflect and think before they answer.

Empathy is another trait to look for when hiring an employee that will strive to succeed. Someone who has empathy is aware of how they act in the workplace. They will be cooperative and try to be as helpful as they can to their co-workers. Hiring an empathetic person doesn't necessarily mean that they are unwilling to make tough decisions in order to hurt someone else's feelings, but rather, they are aware of the impact they have on others, taking other's opinions into consideration. When interviewing a potential employee, ask them how they dealt with angry customers or co-workers in their past work experience. Look for answers like they noticed the co-worker getting upset but decided not to let it affect them when it came to getting a job done. Look for answers based on if this person were to try to help someone or not.

The last thing to look for in an emotionally intelligent employee is their social skills. To possess social skills means to be able to connect with a wide range of people, going beyond friendliness. When someone has social skills, they are great team players and can manage all areas of work tasks due to their ability to work with people or by themselves. These people have high leadership skills and can address problems and conflict appropriately. In an interview, ask the potential employee things that are related to projects and challenges encountered around agendas, temperaments, and influencing people.

Conclusion

So what can we take away from learning about emotional intelligence? Emotional intelligence is the ability to be aware of your emotions alongside the emotions of others. It enables us to act and behave constructively to address situations that arise in our lives. We now know how to be empathetic, self-aware, and manage ourselves in social settings. We understand how being emotionally intelligent can set us up for maximum success and achievement of our goals through self-management. We have also learned how to become emotionally intelligent leaders. In relationships, we recognize, through emotional intelligence, what a healthy environment is like and how to address arguments in an empathetic way. My hopes for you as the reader is that you come out of this practicing all the characteristics of a socially and emotionally intelligent person because I want everyone to succeed and accomplish their hopes and dreams. When we are successful by developing these traits, our environments become more positive, our friends become closer, and our careers become easier. By now, you can start to address, based on this one characteristic, how to envelop the world around you, letting people be influenced by your smart decision-making skills and your powerful outlook on managing stressful events. Ask yourself if your questions have been answered thoroughly and appropriately. Is there anything else you would like to know based on emotional intelligence or EQ? What exactly are you going to put into practice? How will fixing certain things in our life help you become emotionally intelligent? Don't just answer these questions, embrace them and put them into practice starting right now! Be the one person that people look up to, stop hiding in the shadows, and get out in the world to take on what the universe needs you to be - what you need yourself to be.

Again, if you were anything like me, a shy, reserved, innocent human being, then I hope from reading this book you can become more attuned to who you can be. I hope you can develop all of the ways that make you who you are by using emotional intelligence to get ahead. If you want to be successful, you need to take action. Stop making excuses about when the right time to begin, because the time is now. The time for change is in the few short moments after you close this book. Take into account all that you have learned and chase your goals to become the best version of yourself that you know and can be. Emotional intelligence is not just about being successful, it is about fitting into society and overcoming our fears to achieve what we have put off. It is about making a difference in your life, and others' lives around you. So, maybe you don't want to be the center of attention, and perhaps you may just want to stay shy and reserved. That is okay, too, and I will tell you why - Emotional intelligence fits all personalities. You don't just need to be a leader to achieve success; you need to be confident in the way you portray yourself to others. To accomplish that goal, work on being self-aware and understand exactly how to self-regulate your emotions. It's a good thing you just read a whole book about how. Ask yourself, aside from emotional intelligence, what else can I learn about? What more can I understand? How can I set myself up for success? How will knowledge and self-help establish happiness for myself and the people I love? Who else deserves to know about emotional intelligence?

When you correctly identify these aspects of your life, not only can you turn emotional intelligence into whatever it is you decide to accomplish, you can alter your life for what fits your needs the most.

Are you a beginner entrepreneur? Have you just finished high school or college and aren't quite sure what you want to do? Are you a successful businessman and already have an organized company? Perhaps you are an employer seeking emotionally intelligent employees, or maybe you are an employee seeking professional emotionally intelligent employers. Wherever you are, whatever you fit into, and whatever goal you are trying to accomplish, emotional intelligence is a key characteristic to obtain due to the numerous studies of individuals and companies that have become successful by maintaining this strong trait. Ask yourself, what was your mind state before picking up this book? What is your mental state now that you have finished? Do you see a gap? Is there any difference? How have your goals changed? How do you currently view your life as opposed to how you viewed it before? What can you take away? Why? Have I answered all your questions? All of these questions are good to answer and most importantly understand. When we understand things on a deeper level, we can take from our knowledge and use it to benefit ourselves. Knowledge is power, and power is success.

Let's wrap this up. It doesn't matter where you are in your life if you take into account everything you have learned from *Emotional Intelligence;* Mastery Bible for Sales Success and Enhanced Relationships, Discover Why It Can Matter More Than IQ and practice using it in your personality, you will become successful. It may take a while as nothing happens overnight, but it will happen. Even if you are already a successful entrepreneur of some sort, you can never go wrong with learning more and loving yourself for achieving your goals. All in all, developing emotional intelligence can make you a better person and a person others will want to be around. So go ahead, be that person that can greatly influence wide ranges of crowds; be that person that strives to get the most out of life no matter what you are doing or where you are.

Good luck and I hope I have not only impressed you but have made you more aware of what you can accomplish.

Sincerely, **J.P. Edwin**

References

https://www.psychologytoday.com/ca/basics/emotional-intelligence

https://en.wikipedia.org/wiki/Emotional_intelligence

https://en.wikipedia.org/wiki/Emotion#Basic_emotions

https://medium.com/@iamjustincscott/an-introduction-to-emotional-intelligence-eq-dee26ef780dc

https://www.healthline.com/health/emotional-intelligence#components

https://www.inc.com/justin-bariso/13-things-emotionally-intelligent-people-do.html

https://www.inc.com/john-rampton/10-qualities-of-people-with-high-emotional-intelligence.html

https://alanmallory.com/2018/02/emotional-intelligence-importance-self-awareness-self-regulation/

https://www.pathwaytohappiness.com/self-awareness.htm

https://positivepsychologyprogram.com/self-regulation/#psychology-self-regulation

https://www.verywellmind.com/how-you-can-practice-self-regulation-4163536

https://www.success.com/4-changes-you-can-make-to-reach-your-full-potential/

https://www.success.com/6-steps-to-discover-your-true-self/

https://www.success.com/john-c-maxwell-4-steps-to-create-balance-in-your-life/

https://www.success.com/3-techniques-to-never-stop-learning/

https://www.success.com/7-qualities-of-people-with-high-emotional-intelligence/

https://www.special-learning.com/article/performance_intelligence_quotient_piq

https://www.livestrong.com/article/228281-how-to-calculate-your-mental-age/

https://en.wikipedia.org/wiki/Intelligence_quotient

https://www.scmp.com/article/655580/what-more-important-eq-or-iq

https://www.rewireme.com/happiness/emotional-intelligence-important-iq/

https://owlcation.com/social-sciences/Why-Emotional-Intelligence-is-More-Important-

Than-IQ

https://www.rewireme.com/happiness/emotional-intelligence-important-iq/

https://www.encyclopedia.com/social-sciences/dictionaries-thesauruses-pictures-and-press-releases/social-worlds

https://sociology.unc.edu/undergraduate-program/sociology-major/what-is-sociology/

https://www.gottman.com/blog/emotional-intelligence-key-successful-leadership/

https://vidooly.com/blog/emotional-intelligence-for-social-media-marketing/

https://www.verywellmind.com/utilizing-emotional-intelligence-in-the-workplace-4164713

https://www.psychologytoday.com/ca/blog/cutting-edge-leadership/201407/what-is-social-intelligence-why-does-it-matter

https://www.universalclass.com/articles/psychology/the-impact-of-emotional-intelligence-and-personal-relationships.htm

https://www.elitedaily.com/p/does-emotional-intelligence-matter-in-a-relationship-couples-therapists-weigh-in-13113609

https://stylecaster.com/how-to-improve-emotional-iq-of-relationship/

https://www.entrepreneur.com/article/318187

https://www.verywellmind.com/signs-of-low-emotional-intelligence-2795958

https://www.fastcompany.com/3047455/why-emotionally-intelligent-people-are-more-successful